Your journal (

Your journal of Yoga

◆

A journal for yoga teachers to keep track of their yoga classes, lesson plans, personal practice, workshops attended, and much more.

April Farrell-Hasty RYT

iUniverse, Inc.
New York Lincoln Shanghai

Your journal of Yoga
A journal for yoga teachers to keep track of their yoga classes, lesson plans, personal practice, workshops attended, and much more.

Copyright © 2006 by April Farrell-Hasty

All rights reserved. No part of this book may be used or reproduced by any means, graphic, electronic, or mechanical, including photocopying, recording, taping or by any information storage retrieval system without the written permission of the publisher except in the case of brief quotations embodied in critical articles and reviews.

iUniverse books may be ordered through booksellers or by contacting:

iUniverse
2021 Pine Lake Road, Suite 100
Lincoln, NE 68512
www.iuniverse.com
1-800-Authors (1-800-288-4677)

ISBN-13: 978-0-595-37282-9 (pbk)
ISBN-13: 978-0-595-81678-1 (ebk)
ISBN-10: 0-595-37282-1 (pbk)
ISBN-10: 0-595-81678-9 (ebk)

Printed in the United States of America

This book belongs to

_____

If lost please call me my information is below.

_____

_____

Thank you

Read the best books first or you may not have a chance to read them all.
-Henry David Thoreau-

Add the dates of use for this book.
_____
_____

Reality is simply the loss of the ego.
-Shri Ramana Maharishi-

Check the website for updated versions of this book.
www.peacefullotus.com

Intention

"I firmly believe the world will sort itself out in the end.
Believe it with me. At least none of us will be around
To be proven wrong.—Stuart Wilde "The Secrets of Life"

My intention is to have a book that is mat bag size for yoga teachers to carry to class to use for their classes and for themselves. To organize your life related to yoga.

Visit my website
www.peacefullotus.com

"Facts do not cease to exist because they are ignored."

—Aldous Huxley

Contents

Introduction xvii
Yoga teachers Code of ethics xxi

Part One
Teaching the Eight Limbs and Other Yoga Philosophies 3
Pranayama Examples 4
Meditation Examples 9
Kirtan 17
Affirmations 25
Favorite Yoga Sutras Gita, Upanishads Quote, ... 28
Quotes/Info from Articles Write or paste here 31
Partner Yoga 34
Anatomy 38
Pregnancy Yoga 43

Part Two
Lesson Plans 105
Short Lesson Plans 183
Adjustments 236
Student Problem Areas 251
Yoga Cures for Various Problems 268

Part Three

Workshops You Attend 273

A new way to take notes 279

New Asanas you have borrowed from classes or workshops 280

Classes/Workshop Notes 287

Classes I Like 309

Your Yoga Practice 312

Telephone Book 348

Notes 352

About April 361

Acknowledgements

I wish to acknowledge all those yogis who came before me, and to those who brought the practice of yoga where it is today.

I wish to thank my family for their patience. Thanks to my husband, Ron and my children (Bryttani, and Arjay) for encouraging me.

Thanks to E.Z. for making me laugh and smile.

Thanks to my best friend Barbara Forucault who encouraged me to keep going when I was sick and discouraged.

Thanks to Toni Brummond my editor for all your help.

To all my teachers your guidance was appreciated. To all my students, I would not be teaching if it were not for you. Thank you for your trust.

To my Mother in Law, Irene Hasty

To my Mom, Brandy Mitchell

To my Dad, Syl Farrell

Thanks to my four legged friends (dogs), Bodhi and Dino who kept me company as I typed this book. They spent every minute with me.

Thank you to all…. I prostrate…. Gratitude and love.

Om shanti

April

Introduction

This book is for yoga teachers. I hope you find it helpful. I have used it for two years, I love it!

I wrote this book because I truly needed it. I knew this information, but occasionally when I needed a meditation, or someone told me they had back pain I could rattle off one or two asanas for back pain, but I actually knew four to six asana per problem. I could not remember everything when asked. So I compiled a book of asanas and information. I used it for a year I had more information than I planned. I had telephone numbers, email addresses, a summary of what I thought my paycheck should be, based on the students in the class, I had workshop lesson plans for future workshops, and. I had asanas and sequences I had borrowed from other instructors, and much more.

I found it easy to write this book compared to my other two books. This was a labor of love. I sent this book to some of my friends and they recommended I add the yoga practice page, as it is not in my original book. I added the CEU page because I am trying to keep up with my C.E.U.'s, for Yoga Alliance. I knew this would be easy if you are taking notes and this book is with you.

My husband was in the military for 22 years I have studied yoga all over the planet as a military wife. I have studied with famous yogis, infamous yogis and some not so famous yogis. I have learned a lot from everyone. I have changed my destiny because of yoga and I am so grateful to have had the opportunities I have had. When my husband was in the military we moved every two to three years. So I would study one type of yoga move to a different military base and what I was currently studying was not available at the new location. So I took a new type of yoga. I was not able to get certified in anything, because I could not commit to studying a type of yoga until I knew more about it. This took about a year or so for me to familiarize myself with the new yoga. When I finally started training in this new yoga, I moved again. I was so unhappy about this situation!!! Sometimes I studied more than one type of yoga at a time because I liked both styles of yoga equally. I now see I had a very comprehensive yoga education in everything. You name it and I have probably studied it! I became a Yoga Alliance registered teacher in 2002.

I have a hereditary illness, sickle cell anemia and yoga has done so much for me. I could spend two days discussing the benefits I have received from yoga. I have come so far. B.Y. (before yoga) I thought I built a wing on the hospital near my home with all my frequent visits. I was so sick!!!! I should be in the hospital for two weeks get out go home for a few days and be admitted again for another two weeks. I lived like this for years while traveling with the military, with two small children and a husband who was patient, loving beyond belief. I stand corrected this was not living. It was a painful existence. A.Y. (after yoga) I rarely get hospitalized!!!!! I once went five years without hospitalization. I was still ill during this period. I either stayed at home, went to the doctor or I went to the emergency room and was released to my home in a few hours. This improved the quality of my life 150 percent. This is how I currently live. I still have bad days, but they are few and far between.

I have done yoga most of my life actually. But I never really practiced yoga until I was in my late 20's. I did asana, not much pranayama or meditation. When I put it all together I practiced yoga and this is when the changes occurred in my life. I could not connect to the spiritual side of yoga at first. I was confused. I did not know where I belonged spiritually. Most of my 30's I read every religious book I could find. I read the Bible, Upanishads, Vedas, Qu'ran and several other books. I could tell you about being a Sikh, a Quaker, Taoism, Hinduism, and Scientology. I was seeking a reason for my illness, why was I born with a hereditary illness? Why was I so sick? Why, why, why me?

I read Louise Hay, any book on healing. I became a Reiki master. I also became a lay doctor, as a military wife I often moved to places where I was the only sickle cell patient. I could tell the ER staff what I needed in their terminology. Some military doctors had never encountered a patient with my illness. I can read and understand my chart like a doctor. I can read medical shorthand, and I learned the valuable skill of firing a doctor while sick lying in bed. I was seeking an answer, and like most people I had the answer in front of me all the time. When I realized it was not about me. It was what I had chosen to experience.

I would not trade B.Y. for A.Y. for any amount of money. This is not an endorsement that yoga can cure sickle cell anemia or any other illness you may have. (Although a famous yogi cured himself of tuberculosis) This is what yoga and lifestyle changes have done for me. I rarely see the doctor now. I went from seeing my hematologist every four weeks to seeing him every twelve to sixteen weeks for a CBC (complete blood count) to check my h&h (hemoglobin and hematocrit). I now see the acupuncturist, the massage therapist most than I see the allopathic doctor.

I have seen arthritic people feel better with yoga and not be as stiff. I have seen kids with ADD calm down. I have seen elderly people attend yoga class and make friends in class where once they were isolated and lonely couch potatoes. This is not a scientific study although they do exist. This is just my personal experience.

I hope you realize that we as yoga teachers have the power to do what yoga has done for me for other people. Teaching yoga can has become too common place, too trendy. I have seen teachers and teacher trainees at my school who mistakenly think there is money to be made in yoga. There is for the yoga superstars. For most of us it is a struggle, and we all have regular jobs that pay the rent. Most studios are struggling to pay the rent. But know what you are doing for the world is powerful. You are contributing to healing mankind. I think we are going through a growth spurt in human development, and yoga is a part of that growth.

Yoga is sacred to me. I value it and want only the best for yoga's future. I want it to continue to grow and become more popular so others can benefit from it. The future of yoga is in our hands, and I have every confidence that the growth of yoga will continue to grow exponentially. I believe that those of us who carry the torch are yoga teachers for the betterment of all beings.

> "Love What You Do.
> Do What You Love."
> Wayne Dyer…Secrets to Manifesting Your Destiny

Yoga teachers Code of ethics

Several people and yoga organizations have written a code of ethics and this one just summarizes what I believe should not take place between a teacher and a student. As the teacher you have an obligation to create a safe environment for your students.

Teach the student without being overtly critical of their alignment. I feel as long as the student is not doing harm to themselves, don't overly correct them. New students they will not be back if you overly correct them because the class is no longer fun.

Don't overwhelm your students. You want to retain the students you have and have them invite more people to your class. Inspire your students, push them to their limit. Not your limit. This was a mistake I made when I first started teaching. I taught too easy unchallenging classes. Then I taught too difficult classes. You need to find the balance. And you need to teach the people in front of you not the asanas.

Don't cross the line and date your students. I have **never** done this. My students all of us as a group go out to lunch after class. If the entire class goes to lunch it also creates community. And you get to know your students. And they get to know you.

Keep your classes easy, (instructions). Have you ever seen a class with unclear instructions? Everyone is twisting and contorting their bodies to see what they need to do next. Keep your classes fun. Have a sense of humor. Try to remember your student's names. I know my students names, but struggle with new students names. If some one who has come to class less than three times I struggle to remember their name. I have learned to notice the order student arrive and I walk over to the sign up sheet and look at the names on the sheet.

Don't touch your students to correct them without their permission. Some people have issues with being touched. (Rape, incest victims) Some people just do not want to be touched. Always ask.

PART ONE

Teaching the Eight Limbs and Other Yoga Philosophies

Should you teach the yoga sutras, eight limbs, Upanishads? Yes if you do not how will your students learn the concepts of yoga? I start with ahimsa. And ask the student to be kind with themselves tell your students not to force their body into any asana. I explain it more fully and add being kind to others, animals and being a vegetarian. Ironically enough most of my students are vegetarian. Or on the path to being vegetarian.

I quote the yoga sutras, Upanishads and many other things during class, and at the end of class after Savasana. Someone always asks for more information. And I recommend a book or two.

Pranayama Examples

1. I like to do a 3 part breath with kumbuka, (breath retention) then I change to a 4 part breath and I add the kumbuka breath on both ends of the breath. (Beginning of inhale and exhale.) Then I make the inhalations longer than the exhalations, then switch and make the exhalations longer than the inhalations. This is very relaxing. I end class with this prior to Savasana.

2. I begin class with bhastrika a very slow round to warm up and work up to a faster round. Until all total we have done 108. Either do three rounds of 36. Or do smaller rounds of four.

3. Alternate nostril breathing to begin class. Once the room is calmer change the breathing.

4. Evening classes I like to begin with a Savasana so everyone can unwind after work. A short round of pranayama then I am just quiet for a few minutes. The sequence I frequently use is a five part breath, followed by a four part breath, then a 3 part breath. Then I let the student's breath normally for one to two minutes and I repeat the sequence. This takes about eight to ten minutes depending on the students. I watch the rise and fall of their abdomen to determine if they are relaxed.

Pranayama Sequences

Pranayama Sequences

Pranayama Sequences

Pranayama Sequences

"The mind is everything; what you think, you become."
—Buddha

Many teachers do not use meditations; I do breath counting for two minutes after Savasana (counting backwards from 10. If you have a thought start the counting over.). I also do other short meditations.

Meditation Examples

Centering Meditations
Counting backwards from 10 or 20 you count slowly, slowly.

Tonglen- Practice of taking in some one's pain, putting your self in the others persons shoes. Giving and receiving compassion meditation.
This meditation helps you effectively deal with any emotion or pain in your life. I use it to deal with negative emotions and feelings. You can also use this meditation to deal with a problem relationship in your life. Put yourself in their shoes.

Sit up straight or remain lying down (after Savasana) take a few deep breaths. Come into a meditative state and feel the emotion you are feeling. (Anger, jealousy etc.) Think about how many other people in the world are having these thoughts and feelings. Know that you are not alone in what you are feeling. Take these feeling into your heart and hold the thoughts in your heart. The time will vary for each person. Until you really feel it. I recommend no more than one minute. And release the feeling from your heart.

Remember other people feel this emotion. This will free you to recognize that regardless of sex, age, race, and socioeconomic status we are all the same. We all feel the same emotions. And that you are not alone. Taking your pain or someone else's pain into your heart or feeling their emotions will result in more compassion for yourself and for others.

Chakra Meditation
First use progressive relaxation then move up through the chakras. This is just an **example** of how I begin. Go through all the chakras.

1. Muldhara - Survival chakra
Sound Lam (pronounced Lum)
Yellow I then have the student see the chakra, feel the energy, and visualize vibrating the chakra clockwise.
Then do each chakra, I spend a few minutes on each chakra.

Death meditation

The Sufis say you must die before you die. Buddhism has Powa Yoga teachers have the death meditation. Only do this meditation with experienced students. Once you have experienced death you are no longer afraid of it. It is freeing and very emotional for most students. Just take your students through a gentle peaceful death, and burial. Explain to them in the gentlest way. Another reason I do it is the body is temporary, yet so many people are fixated on their bodies. Botox, plastic surgery, diets, weight loss, we are only here temporarily. This meditation helps students remember the body is impermanent. In all the years I have done death meditation I have had four students come back and tell me they were in a situation where they thought they were dying. (Car accident, heart attack, etc.) And their mind came back to the death meditation and it put them at peace. They were not afraid any more.

To teach the death meditation you need to have experienced it first. I would also recommend that you be an energy worker. A lot of powerful emotions are brought up and sometimes energies need to be balanced and calmed. If you do Reiki throw the symbols during the meditation for everyone's highest good.

Start with a body scan or yoga nidra and get everyone into a receptive state to help calm them down. Go to the students fear. (Most are auto accidents, drowning, and fire.) Go slowly and tell your students if it is too intense to leave the room. Walk them through several scenarios. And allow them to face their fears. Do no more than five students at a time. There is no right way to do this. However there is a wrong way. Remember to be sensitive, compassionate and try it first yourself!

Psycho—neuro Immunology Meditations

I do this with my private students primarily.
I used to teach a class for women with or recovering from breast cancer. Some women had just had surgery; some were losing the battle. I would come to them and meditate with them free of charge. I would be as gentle or aggressive as they could handle. I used meditation, affirmations, and visualization to help. One of

my yoga teachers was ill and I did this with her. She appreciated it, but warned me do not do this with yoga teachers, as they prefer pranayama. But she found it helpful and continued it on her own. I must admit in my experience yoga teachers only want mediation and pranayama. But students do not know what they need and they find my gentle affirmations and mediations helpful. **I only do this when I am asked by a student.**

Meditations

Meditations

Meditations

Mantra and Kritan Examples

"Man" meaning to think tra" meaning tool or instrument. Mantra literal meaning is tool of thought. Mantras are phrases, symbols, religious words that are repeated for chosen period of time to bring about a desired result. Some mantras are to attract mate, to bring wealth. Most are for spiritual purposes to purify the body. Traditionally mantras are repeated 125,000 times. If you repeat your mantra twice a day for 30 minutes it could be repeated 125.000 times. Mantras can also be written or taped. It has been my experience that people either enjoy kirtan or do not. There is no neutrality. Because most of my students are uncomfortable with it, I stick to Om primarily. I have noticed most advanced yoga students enjoy chanting. Kirtan is chanting.

Mantra

Om

Om Shanti, Shanti, Shanti
Om Peace, peace, peace

Sat Nam
I am truth

Namah Shivaya
Homage to Shiva

Lokah Samasta Sukhino Bhavantu
May all beings be happy and free

Guru Brahma
Guru Vishnu
Guru Devo Maheshwara
Guru Sak Shat
Param Brahma
Tash Mayi Shri Guruvay Namaha
Tash Mayi Shri Guruvay Namaha

Our creation is that Guru,
The duration of our lives is that Guru,
Our trials and the death of the body is that Guru,
There is a Guru that is near by,
And a Guru that is beyond the beyond.
I offer all of myself to the Guru

Mantra and Kritan Examples

Kirtan

It this is not comfortable for you. Remember you cannot teach what you do not practice.

Sita Rama Rama Ram Sita Ram. Sita Ram Ram Ram. Hare Krishna Hare Krishna Khrishna Krishna Hare Hare. Hare Rama Hare Rama Rama Rama Hare Hare

Hanuman Chalisa (very long)

Mantra & Kirtan

Mantra & Kirtan

Mantra & Kirtan

Mantra & Kirtan

Mantra & Kirtan

Mantra & Kirtan

Mantra & Kirtan

Affirmations

Some of my students are ill or have special needs and I address these needs at the end of Savasana with affirmations. I have them repeat them quietly to themselves. Also if I have new students I just announce it is time for your affirmations and my students repeat them quietly to themselves. Several teachers do not use affirmations, and for those of you who do not I am sure you will find another use for this page.

For Example
I am centered and peaceful all the time.

Affirmations

Affirmations

Favorite Yoga Sutras Gita, Upanishads Quote,

This is one of my favorites although it is from a yoga teacher.

"All the eight limbs of yoga are in one pose."
Patricia Walden

Favorite Yoga Sutras, Gita, Upanishads Quote

Favorite Sutras, Gita, Upanishads Quote

Quotes/Info from Articles
Write or paste here

Quotes/Info from Articles
Write or paste here

Quotes/Info from Articles
Write or paste here

Partner Yoga

I sometimes do partner yoga at special events. Retreats I do always begin with partner yoga so everyone gets to meet the other participants. We form two lines of people and each person does one partner yoga asana with the person across from them and then we switch asanas and people. I also do a partner yoga class for Valentine Day, Mothers Day, and Fathers Day. I call it Bring Mom to Yoga! But most times Mom brings the kids or hubby.

Partner Yoga

Partner Yoga

Partner Yoga

Anatomy

Add any anatomy information you feel you need to remember. I actually had new information I learned.

Here is something to get you started.

The spine vertebra is numbered from top to bottom in each region
Cervical vertebrae C-1 to C-7 neck

Thoracic vertebra T-1 to T-12 moves ribs

Lumbar L1 to L5 Large weight bearing

Sacrum S-1 to S-5 pelvic

Coccyx tailbone

Lordosis curvature of the lumbar

Kyphosis curvature of thoracic

Scoliosis abnormal lateral curvature of thoracic

Anatomy

Anatomy

Anatomy

Anatomy

Pregnancy Yoga

I do not teach prenatal yoga; although I have had long time students become pregnant and want to continue. I will see them for the class they come to and tell me they are expecting. After that I will not see them. I explain that I am not certified in prenatal yoga.

I find that prenatal yoga is more than I am willing to do. Pregnant students are limited to what they can do by the trimester they are currently in. I refer the student to the prenatal class and tell them to also ask their friends to recommend a teacher as well. Check with their doctor before attending class. I also ask them to wait until the first trimester is over before starting class, because this is when the fetus is most likely to separate from the placenta.

Find a class that meets their level of physical activity.

I have often found resistance to leaving my class. I tell my students this is when you need a prenatal class. It can help you meet other moms and find out information about baby products, doctors, etc…I always stay in contact with the student, attend the baby shower, and I crochet or knit a gift if I have time. Otherwise I buy something to fit the student's personality…

Asanas that cannot be done by pregnant students

1. No twist
2. No lying on the abdomen (cobra/up dog)
3. No upside down asanas. (It can be done by experienced yogis, but I would not allow a student to do it.) Viparita Karani, for no more than 3 minutes (legs up the wall) would be fine.

Pregnancy Yoga

Pregnancy Yoga

Asanas for Neck & Shoulders

Asanas for Neck & Shoulders

Asanas for Neck & Shoulders

Asanas for Back pain

Asanas for Back Pain

Asanas for Back Pain

Asanas for Back Pain

Asanas for Back Pain

Asanas for Abs

You need asanas for abs to create a strong back. You need to work opposing muscle groups.

Asanas for Abs

Asanas for Abs

Asanas for Abs

Asanas for Tight Hamstrings

Asanas for Tight Hamstrings

Asanas for Tight Hamstrings

Asanas for Tight Hamstrings

Asanas for Hip Openers

Asanas for Hip Openers

Asanas for Hip Openers

Asanas for Hip Openers

Asanas for Hip Openers

Asanas for Hip Openers

Your Asanas for_____

Your Asanas for_____

Your Asanas for _____

Your Asanas for_____

Your Asanas for_____

Surya Namascar

Add your different versions of Sun Salutations

Surya Namascar

Surya Namascar

Surya Namascar

Surya Namascar

Surya Namascar

Lunar (moon) & Earth Salutations

Lunar (moon) & Earth Salutations

Lunar (moon) & Earth Salutations

Lunar (moon) & Earth Salutations

My Workshops
Name of workshop_____
Date_____

Add your lesson plans for workshops you teach

My Workshops
Workshop_____
Date _____

My Workshops
Workshop_____
Date _____

My Workshops
Workshop_____

Date _____

My Workshops
Workshop_____
Date _____

My Workshops
Workshop_____
Date_____

My Workshops
Workshop_____

Date _____

My Workshops
Workshop_____

Date _____

My Workshops
Workshop_____
Date_____

My Workshops
Workshop_____
Date _____

Opening Sequences

Themes

For my classes I like to have a theme each week I try to have the themes related in some way then I move on to something else.

Theme

Digestive Yoga
Abdominal yoga
Asanas you don't think of as a twist
Revolved asanas. (Triangle, side angle, half moon all revolved)
This would include twist (seated, standing, lying down)

Theme

Inversions
Adho Mukha Svanasana
Teaching Adho Mukha Vrksasana and Salamba Sirsasana
(Headstand and handstand)
Vipariti Karani Legs up the wall
Asanas you don't think of as inversions

Your Journal of Yoga
Lesson Plans
To make the class longer repeat each side more or hold for longer breaths after the warm up.

Forward Bends to work tight hamstrings.
Stand in Tadasana (mountain)
Inhale arms up, exhale down uttanasana (standing forward fold) hold 3-5 breaths
Repeat 4 times

Stand in Tadasana (mountain)
Inhale arms up, exhale down hold 3-5 breaths
Step one leg back into a lunge hold 3-5 breaths
Repeat other side
Total of 2 times each side.

Half Surya Namascar (sun salutes) as many times as you want.
I would do four.

Legs wide apart Prasarita Padottanasana fold forward hold 3 breaths then place one hand on the floor in the center of your chest
Spiral the other arm up into a twisting triangle.
Repeat on each side twice.

With legs wide apart Prasarita Padottanasana
Right arm to your right hip left arm to your right ankle or foot, then move the hand on your ankle and stretch it out in front of you.
Repeat on each side 2 times.

Arch your back up to standing position one vertebrae at a time.
Stand in tadasana. Then stand at the front of your mat step one foot back and come into Parsvottanasana hold for 3-5 breaths repeat on each side twice.

Step into Adho Mukha Svanasana (downward facing dog) hold for 3-5 breaths.
Walk back into uttanasana

Stand for vrksasana (tree) once on each side. Then come into virabhadrasana III on each side.

Sit into Dandasana hold for 3-5 breaths inhale arms up, exhale into Paschimottanasana (seated forward fold) hold for 3-5 breaths Add Marichyasana I for 3-5 breaths.

Janu Sirsasana (head to knee forward fold)

Extend the legs wide fold forward into Upavistha Konasana. Add a supine twist then move into Supta Padangusthasana reclining big toe pose.

Cool down and end the class any way you want. Corpse pose and pranayama

Your Journal of Yoga
Lesson Plans
To make the class longer repeat each side more or hold for longer breaths
Twist to ease the digestion.

Start class with Surya Namascar as many as you choose (I would do 4-6 to warm up)

Do a standing twist. Stand at the front of your mat step the right foot back inhale the arms up to shoulder height, left arm in front. Then change the arms so the right arm is in front by twisting and looking back at the back hand. Hold 3-5 breaths. Repeat on each side twice.

Parivrtta Parsvakonasana (revolved side angle) hold 5 breaths. Repeat on each side three times. Come into Trikonasana (triangle pose) then transition into Parivrtta Trikonasana and hold 5 breaths. **If you have a beginning student just have them do trikonasana and hold for 3 breaths.**

Ardha Chandrasana for a beginner and Parivrtta Ardha Chandrasana for a more advanced student.

Utkatasana (chair) and twist one arm behind you one in front of you, turn and look at the back arm hold 3-5 breaths.

Do any balancing asanas you choose.

Then have a seat and come into a seated twist of your choice repeat twice on each side.

On all fours walk hands to the right hold this twist for 5 breaths and then walk hands to the left hold five breaths. Repeat. Do cat/cow a few times.

Come onto your knees, and do Ustrasana (camel) for an advanced student do Ustrasana twist holding the opposite ankle or heel the other arm in the air. Repeat twice on each side hold for 3-5 breaths.

Have your students lie on their backs and come into halasana (plow)

Matsyasana (fish) hold for 5 breaths.
Include a few supine twists then bring both knees to the chest and hold.

Cool down and end the class any way you want add Salamba Sarvangasana (shoulder stand)

Corpse pose and pranayama

Your Journal of Yoga
Lesson Plans
To make the class longer repeat each side more or hold for longer breaths

Backbends

Start on all fours
Cat/Cow repeat several times.

Stay on all fours come to a flat back extend the right leg and he left arm hold 3 breaths then bend the right leg and hold with the left arm for three breaths. Change sides and repeat twice.

On all fours walk hands to the right hold this twist for 5 breaths and then walk hands to the center and to the left hold five breaths. Repeat. Do cat/cow a few times. Then come into Adho Mukha Svanasana, and bend the knees, then straighten the knees. Do this a few times to warm up and lengthen the back and the legs.

Lie on the abdomen and come into Bhujangasana (cobra) hold for 3-5 breaths. Sit in Balasana and repeat Bhujangasana. **Stronger students can do Urdhva Mukha Svanasana.**

Lie on the abdomen lift the legs for 3-5 breaths repeat four times.

Lie on the abdomen and come into Dhanurasana (bow) hold 3-5 breaths, come into balasana then repeat Dhanurasana.

Sit in balasana for 6 deep breaths.

Lie on your back and come into Setu Bandha Sarvangasana (bridge) and repeat several times. Then bring both knees to your chest and roll your back out.

Lie on your back and come back into Setu Bandha Sarvangasana or for more advanced students have them do Urdhva Dhanurasana (wheel).
Come onto knees and do Parighasana (Gate Pose).

Stand and do any balance asanas you choose. Try to add Natarajasana (it is a back bend)

Stand in tadasana and do standing camel with hands on the low back. Counter pose with Parsvottanasana.

Adho Mukha Svanasana (downward facing dog) hold for 5 breaths, lift the right leg up and swing it forward into Rajakapotasana (pigeon) advanced students can do Eka Pada Rajakapotasana. Step back into down dog and repeat the other side, twice total.

Lie on back for Setu bandha sarvangasana and cool down and end class any way you choose. Corpse pose and pranayama

Your Journal of Yoga
Lesson Plans
To make the class longer repeat each side more or hold for longer breaths. I prefer to repeat each side twice.

My Balance Challenge Workshop
Stand in tadasana
Do half Surya Namascar six times. Followed by Surya Namascar four times. Come into Uttanasana and stand on hands for five breaths.

Have the class come into Adho Mukha Svanasana to Bhujangasana or Urdhva Mukha Svanasana, and back to Adho Mukha Svanasana hold each asana 4 breaths then move to the next. Repeat this 5 times.

Stand in tadasana transition into vrksasana, move the hands into various positions. Then lean to the right and lean to the left. Stand in tadasana. Repeat this sequence several times.

Come into Virabhadrasana I for 5 breaths transition into Virabhadrasana II for 5 breaths then reverse Virabhadrasana I for 5 breaths transition into Virabhadrasana III for 5 breaths transition into standing splits for 3 breaths. Repeat each side 2 times.

Rest in Tadasana

Come into Virabhadrasana III transition into Ardha Chandrasana (Half Moon Pose) and advanced students can add Parivrtta Ardha Chandrasana (Revolved Half Moon Pose) then come back into virabhadrasana III. Breathe into each asana for 3-5 breaths repeat this on each side twice.

Rest in Tadasana

Garudasana (Eagle Pose), to Natarajasana (Lord of the Dance Pose) without letting your leg touch the ground. Repeat each side twice.

Rest in Tadasana

Standing twist to Trikonasana or Parivrtta Trikonasana, to Parsvakonasana (Side Angle Pose) or Parivrtta Parsvakonasana (Revolved Side Angle Pose)

Rest in Tadasana

Paripurna Navasana (Full Boat Pose)

Add any asanas you want to here
Have the class come into Salamba Sarvangasana (shoulder stand) with legs in garudasana if possible then into halasana. End with Viparita Karani (Legs-Up-the-Wall Pose Corpse pose and pranayama

Part Two

Lesson Plans

Lesson Plans are to be written under where you wrote the date on the lesson plan pages. I draw stick people and the space works well for me. I realize some teachers only teach one style of yoga. (Ashtanga, Bikram etc.) So I have sectioned the book for these subtle differences. The short lesson plans are for you. They are after your lesson plans.

I have found in testing the book, the short lesson plan section if you don't need it can be used for morning and evening classes. To separate what you have done in each class. I wanted to give you six months of every category but had I done so this book would not fit into your mat bag

I am thinking of adding a palm OS version on my website. Please email me and tell me what other pages will fit your needs, so I can add them in the next addition of the book.
peacefulotus@yahoo.com

Your Lesson Plans

Draw stick people to write your lesson plan below.

Music played in class today_____ Focus of Class_____

Date_____

Students attending today_____

_____

Total students_____ Estimated paycheck_____ New Students _____

Your Lesson Plans

Music played in class today_____ Focus of Class_____

Date_____

Students attending today_____

_____

Total students_____ Estimated paycheck_____ New Students _____

Your Lesson Plans

Music played in class today_____ Focus of Class_____

Date_____

Students attending today_____

_____

Total students_____ Estimated paycheck_____ New Students _____

Your Lesson Plans

Music played in class today_____ Focus of Class_____

Date_____

Students attending today_____

_____

Total students_____ Estimated paycheck_____ New Students _____

Your Lesson Plans

Music played in class today_____ Focus of Class_____

Date_____

Students attending today_____

_____

Total students_____ Estimated paycheck_____ New Students _____

Your Lesson Plans

Music played in class today_____ Focus of Class_____

Date_____

Students attending today_____

_____

Total students_____ Estimated paycheck_____ New Students _____

Your Lesson Plans

Music played in class today_____ Focus of Class_____

Date_____

Students attending today_____

_____

Total students_____ Estimated paycheck_____ New Students _____

Your Lesson Plans

Music played in class today_____ Focus of Class_____

Date_____

Students attending today_____

_____

Total students_____ Estimated paycheck_____ New Students _____

Your Lesson Plans

Music played in class today_____ Focus of Class_____

Date_____

Students attending today_____

_____

Total students_____ Estimated paycheck_____ New Students _____

Your Lesson Plans

Music played in class today_____ Focus of Class_____

Date_____

Students attending today_____

_____

Total students_____ Estimated paycheck_____ New Students _____

Your Lesson Plans

Music played in class today_____ Focus of Class_____

Date_____

Students attending today_____

_____

Total students_____ Estimated paycheck_____ New Students _____

Your Lesson Plans

Music played in class today_____ Focus of Class_____

Date_____

Students attending today_____

_____

Total students_____ Estimated paycheck_____ New Students _____

Your Lesson Plans

Music played in class today_____ Focus of Class_____

Date_____

Students attending today_____

_____

Total students_____ Estimated paycheck_____ New Students _____

Your Lesson Plans

Music played in class today_____ Focus of Class_____

Date_____

Students attending today_____

_____

Total students_____ Estimated paycheck_____ New Students _____

Your Lesson Plans

Music played in class today_____ Focus of Class_____

Date_____

Students attending today_____

_____

Total students_____ Estimated paycheck_____ New Students _____

Your Lesson Plans

Music played in class today_____ Focus of Class_____

Date_____

Students attending today_____

_____

Total students_____ Estimated paycheck_____ New Students _____

Your Lesson Plans

Music played in class today_____ Focus of Class_____

Date_____

Students attending today_____

_____

Total students_____ Estimated paycheck_____ New Students _____

Your Lesson Plans

Music played in class today_____ Focus of Class_____

Date_____

Students attending today_____

_____

Total students_____ Estimated paycheck_____ New Students _____

Your Lesson Plans

Music played in class today_____ Focus of Class_____

Date_____

Students attending today_____

_____

Total students_____ Estimated paycheck_____ New Students _____

Your Lesson Plans

Music played in class today_____ Focus of Class_____

Date_____

Students attending today_____

_____

Total students_____ Estimated paycheck_____ New Students _____

Your Lesson Plans

Music played in class today_____ Focus of Class_____

Date_____

Students attending today_____

_____

Total students_____ Estimated paycheck_____ New Students _____

Your Lesson Plans

Music played in class today_____ Focus of Class_____

Date_____

Students attending today_____

_____

Total students_____ Estimated paycheck_____ New Students _____

Your Lesson Plans

Music played in class today_____ Focus of Class_____

Date_____

Students attending today_____

_____

Total students_____ Estimated paycheck_____ New Students _____

Your Lesson Plans

Music played in class today_____ Focus of Class_____

Date_____

Students attending today_____

_____

Total students_____ Estimated paycheck_____ New Students _____

Your Lesson Plans

Music played in class today_____ Focus of Class_____

Date_____

Students attending today_____

_____

Total students_____ Estimated paycheck_____ New Students _____

Your Lesson Plans

Music played in class today_____ Focus of Class_____

Date_____

Students attending today_____

_____

Total students_____ Estimated paycheck_____ New Students _____

Your Lesson Plans

Music played in class today_____ Focus of Class_____

Date_____

Students attending today_____

_____

Total students_____ Estimated paycheck_____ New Students _____

Your Lesson Plans

Music played in class today_____ Focus of Class_____

Date_____

Students attending today_____

_____

Total students_____ Estimated paycheck_____ New Students _____

Your Lesson Plans

Music played in class today_____ Focus of Class_____

Date_____

Students attending today_____

_____

Total students_____ Estimated paycheck_____ New Students _____

Your Lesson Plans

Music played in class today_____ Focus of Class_____

Date_____

Students attending today_____

_____

Total students_____ Estimated paycheck_____ New Students _____

Your Lesson Plans

Music played in class today_____ Focus of Class_____

Date_____

Students attending today_____

_____

Total students_____ Estimated paycheck_____ New Students _____

Your Lesson Plans

Music played in class today_____ Focus of Class_____

Date_____

Students attending today_____

_____

Total students_____ Estimated paycheck_____ New Students _____

Your Lesson Plans

Music played in class today_____ Focus of Class_____

Date_____

Students attending today_____

_____

Total students_____ Estimated paycheck_____ New Students _____

Your Lesson Plans

Music played in class today_____ Focus of Class_____

Date_____

Students attending today_____

_____

Total students_____ Estimated paycheck_____ New Students _____

Your Lesson Plans

Music played in class today_____ Focus of Class_____

Date_____

Students attending today_____

_____

Total students_____ Estimated paycheck_____ New Students _____

Your Lesson Plans

Music played in class today_____ Focus of Class_____

Date_____

Students attending today_____

_____

Total students_____ Estimated paycheck_____ New Students _____

Your Lesson Plans

Music played in class today_____ Focus of Class_____

Date_____

Students attending today_____

_____

Total students_____ Estimated paycheck_____ New Students _____

Your Lesson Plans

Music played in class today_____ Focus of Class_____

Date_____

Students attending today_____

_____

Total students_____ Estimated paycheck_____ New Students _____

Your Lesson Plans

Music played in class today_____ Focus of Class_____

Date_____

Students attending today_____

_____

Total students_____ Estimated paycheck_____ New Students _____

Your Lesson Plans

Music played in class today_____ Focus of Class_____

Date_____

Students attending today_____

_____

Total students_____ Estimated paycheck_____ New Students _____

Your Lesson Plans

Music played in class today_____ Focus of Class_____

Date_____

Students attending today_____

_____

Total students_____ Estimated paycheck_____ New Students _____

Your Lesson Plans

Music played in class today_____ Focus of Class_____

Date_____

Students attending today_____

_____

Total students_____ Estimated paycheck_____ New Students _____

Your Lesson Plans

Music played in class today_____ Focus of Class_____

Date_____

Students attending today_____

_____

Total students_____ Estimated paycheck_____ New Students _____

Your Lesson Plans

Music played in class today_____ Focus of Class_____

Date_____

Students attending today_____

_____

Total students_____ Estimated paycheck_____ New Students _____

Your Lesson Plans

Music played in class today_____ Focus of Class_____

Date_____

Students attending today_____

_____

Total students_____ Estimated paycheck_____ New Students _____

Your Lesson Plans

Music played in class today_____ Focus of Class_____

Date_____

Students attending today_____

_____

Total students_____ Estimated paycheck_____ New Students _____

Your Lesson Plans

Music played in class today_____ Focus of Class_____

Date_____

Students attending today_____

_____

Total students_____ Estimated paycheck_____ New Students _____

Your Lesson Plans

Music played in class today_____ Focus of Class_____

Date_____

Students attending today_____

_____

Total students_____ Estimated paycheck_____ New Students _____

Your Lesson Plans

Music played in class today_____ Focus of Class_____

Date_____

Students attending today_____

_____

Total students_____ Estimated paycheck_____ New Students _____

Your Lesson Plans

Music played in class today_____ Focus of Class_____

Date_____

Students attending today_____

_____

Total students_____ Estimated paycheck_____ New Students _____

Your Lesson Plans

Music played in class today_____ Focus of Class_____

Date_____

Students attending today_____

_____

Total students_____ Estimated paycheck_____ New Students _____

Your Lesson Plans

Music played in class today_____ Focus of Class_____

Date_____

Students attending today_____

_____

Total students_____ Estimated paycheck_____ New Students _____

Your Lesson Plans

Music played in class today_____ Focus of Class_____

Date_____

Students attending today_____

_____

Total students_____ Estimated paycheck_____ New Students _____

Your Lesson Plans

Music played in class today_____ Focus of Class_____

Date_____

Students attending today_____

_____

Total students_____ Estimated paycheck_____ New Students _____

Your Lesson Plans

Music played in class today_____ Focus of Class_____

Date_____

Students attending today_____

_____

Total students_____ Estimated paycheck_____ New Students _____

Your Lesson Plans

Music played in class today_____ Focus of Class_____

Date_____

Students attending today_____
_____

Total students_____ Estimated paycheck_____ New Students _____

Your Lesson Plans

Music played in class today_____ Focus of Class_____

Date_____

Students attending today_____

_____

Total students_____ Estimated paycheck_____ New Students _____

Your Lesson Plans

Music played in class today_____ Focus of Class_____

Date_____

Students attending today_____

_____

Total students_____ Estimated paycheck_____ New Students _____

Your Lesson Plans

Music played in class today_____ Focus of Class_____

Date_____

Students attending today_____

_____

Total students_____ Estimated paycheck_____ New Students _____

Your Lesson Plans

Music played in class today_____ Focus of Class_____

Date_____

Students attending today_____

_____

Total students_____ Estimated paycheck_____ New Students _____

Your Lesson Plans

Music played in class today_____ Focus of Class_____

Date_____

Students attending today_____

_____

Total students_____ Estimated paycheck_____ New Students _____

Your Lesson Plans

Music played in class today_____ Focus of Class_____

Date_____

Students attending today_____

_____

Total students_____ Estimated paycheck_____ New Students _____

Your Lesson Plans

Music played in class today_____ Focus of Class_____

Date_____

Students attending today_____

_____

Total students_____ Estimated paycheck_____ New Students _____

Your Lesson Plans

Music played in class today_____ Focus of Class_____

Date_____

Students attending today_____

_____

Total students_____ Estimated paycheck_____ New Students _____

Your Lesson Plans

Music played in class today_____ Focus of Class_____

Date_____

Students attending today_____

_____

Total students_____ Estimated paycheck_____ New Students _____

Your Lesson Plans

Music played in class today_____ Focus of Class_____

Date_____

Students attending today_____

_____

Total students_____ Estimated paycheck_____ New Students _____

Your Lesson Plans

Music played in class today_____ Focus of Class_____

Date_____

Students attending today_____

_____

Total students_____ Estimated paycheck_____ New Students _____

Your Lesson Plans

Music played in class today_____ Focus of Class_____

Date_____

Students attending today_____

_____

Total students_____ Estimated paycheck_____ New Students _____

Your Lesson Plans

Music played in class today_____ Focus of Class_____

Date_____

Students attending today_____

_____

Total students_____ Estimated paycheck_____ New Students _____

Your Lesson Plans

Music played in class today_____ Focus of Class_____

Date_____

Students attending today_____

_____

Total students_____ Estimated paycheck_____ New Students _____

Your Lesson Plans

Music played in class today_____ Focus of Class_____

Date_____

Students attending today_____

_____

Total students_____ Estimated paycheck_____ New Students _____

Your Lesson Plans

Music played in class today_____ Focus of Class_____

Date_____

Students attending today_____

_____

Total students_____ Estimated paycheck_____ New Students _____

Your Lesson Plans

Music played in class today_____ Focus of Class_____

Date_____

Students attending today_____

_____

Total students_____ Estimated paycheck_____ New Students _____

Your Lesson Plans

Music played in class today_____ Focus of Class_____

Date_____

Students attending today_____

_____

Total students_____ Estimated paycheck_____ New Students _____

Your Lesson Plans

Music played in class today_____ Focus of Class_____

Date_____

Students attending today_____

_____

Total students_____ Estimated paycheck_____ New Students _____

Your Lesson Plans

Music played in class today_____ Focus of Class_____

Date_____

Students attending today_____

_____

Total students_____ Estimated paycheck_____ New Students _____

Aromatherapy for Yoga

Essential oil can be used to balance your yoga practice. I sometimes wear lavender oil highly diluted to class. However it is not always appropriate in class because some students are highly sensitive. I would wear oil at home in my daily practice. Essential oils are also used in Ayurveda. There are several combinations for each dosha, these are used to ground and balance the individual. Some yoga studios burns incense or use candles.

Essential Oils used in yoga most often are jasmine, lavender, and sandalwood. An Ayurvedic technique, these oils are heated slightly and used to anoint. They are poured over the third eye chakra as in Shirodhara. Make sure you dilute essential oils with carrier oil.

Lavender oil
Calms, relaxes and soothes the mind and body.

Jasmine Oil
Calming, aids in depression, and is great for blending.

Sandalwood Oil
Grounding, balancing and can be used for meditation. I also like **sandalwood powder** (only high quality) mixed with water. And put the sandalwood power on the pulse points, or the third eye.

Short Lesson Plans

The next several pages are for teachers who teach a style of yoga that is repetitive (Ashtanga primary series, secondary series, Bikram) or use these pages if you do not need a lesson plan.

Music played in class today_____

Date_____

Students attending today_____

_____

Total students_____   Estimated Paycheck _____

Music played in class today_____

Date_____

Students attending today_____

_____

Total students_____   Estimated Paycheck _____

Music played in class today_____

Date_____

Students attending today_____

_____

Total students_____   Estimated Paycheck _____

Music played in class today_____

Date_____

Students attending today_____

_____

Total students_____   Estimated Paycheck _____

Music played in class today_____

Date_____

Students attending today_____

_____

Total students_____   Estimated Paycheck _____

Music played in class today_____

Date_____

Students attending today_____

_____

Total students_____   Estimated Paycheck _____

Music played in class today_____

Date_____

Students attending today_____

_____

Total students_____   Estimated Paycheck _____

Music played in class today_____

Date_____

Students attending today_____

_____

Total students_____   Estimated Paycheck _____

Music played in class today_____

Date_____

Students attending today_____

_____

Total students_____   Estimated Paycheck _____

Music played in class today_____

Date_____

Students attending today_____

_____

Total students_____   Estimated Paycheck _____

Music played in class today_____

Date_____

Students attending today_____

_____

Total students_____   Estimated Paycheck _____

Music played in class today _____

Date _____

Students attending today _____

_____

Total students _____   Estimated Paycheck _____

Music played in class today _____

Date _____

Students attending today _____

_____

Total students _____   Estimated Paycheck _____

Music played in class today _____

Date _____

Students attending today _____

_____

Total students _____   Estimated Paycheck _____

Music played in class today _____

Date _____

Students attending today _____

_____

Total students _____   Estimated Paycheck _____

Music played in class today_____

Date_____

Students attending today_____

_____

Total students_____   Estimated Paycheck _____

Music played in class today_____

Date_____

Students attending today_____

_____

Total students_____   Estimated Paycheck _____

Music played in class today_____

Date_____

Students attending today_____

_____

Total students_____   Estimated Paycheck _____

Music played in class today_____

Date_____

Students attending today_____

_____

Total students_____   Estimated Paycheck _____

Music played in class today_____

Date_____

Students attending today_____

_____

Total students_____   Estimated Paycheck _____

Music played in class today_____

Date_____

Students attending today_____

_____

Total students_____   Estimated Paycheck _____

Music played in class today_____

Date_____

Students attending today_____

_____

Total students_____   Estimated Paycheck _____

Music played in class today_____

Date_____

Students attending today_____

_____

Total students_____   Estimated Paycheck _____

Music played in class today _____

Date _____

Students attending today _____

_____

Total students _____   Estimated Paycheck _____

Music played in class today _____

Date _____

Students attending today _____

_____

Total students _____   Estimated Paycheck _____

Music played in class today _____

Date _____

Students attending today _____

_____

Total students _____   Estimated Paycheck _____

Music played in class today _____

Date _____

Students attending today _____

_____

Total students _____   Estimated Paycheck _____

Music played in class today_____

Date_____

Students attending today_____

_____

Total students_____   Estimated Paycheck _____

Music played in class today_____

Date_____

Students attending today_____

_____

Total students_____   Estimated Paycheck _____

Music played in class today_____

Date_____

Students attending today_____

_____

Total students_____   Estimated Paycheck _____

Music played in class today_____

Date_____

Students attending today_____

_____

Total students_____   Estimated Paycheck _____

Music played in class today_____

Date_____

Students attending today_____

_____

Total students_____   Estimated Paycheck _____

Music played in class today_____

Date_____

Students attending today_____

_____

Total students_____   Estimated Paycheck _____

Music played in class today_____

Date_____

Students attending today_____

_____

Total students_____   Estimated Paycheck _____

Music played in class today_____

Date_____

Students attending today_____

_____

Total students_____   Estimated Paycheck _____

Music played in class today_____

Date_____

Students attending today_____

_____

Total students_____   Estimated Paycheck _____

Music played in class today_____

Date_____

Students attending today_____

_____

Total students_____   Estimated Paycheck _____

Music played in class today_____

Date_____

Students attending today_____

_____

Total students_____   Estimated Paycheck _____

Music played in class today_____

Date_____

Students attending today_____

_____

Total students_____   Estimated Paycheck _____

Music played in class today_____

Date_____

Students attending today_____

_____

Total students_____   Estimated Paycheck _____

Music played in class today_____

Date_____

Students attending today_____

_____

Total students_____   Estimated Paycheck _____

Music played in class today_____

Date_____

Students attending today_____

_____

Total students_____   Estimated Paycheck _____

Music played in class today_____

Date_____

Students attending today_____

_____

Total students_____   Estimated Paycheck _____

Music played in class today_____

Date_____

Students attending today_____

_____

Total students_____   Estimated Paycheck _____

Music played in class today_____

Date_____

Students attending today_____

_____

Total students_____   Estimated Paycheck _____

Music played in class today_____

Date_____

Students attending today_____

_____

Total students_____   Estimated Paycheck _____

Music played in class today_____

Date_____

Students attending today_____

_____

Total students_____   Estimated Paycheck _____

Music played in class today_____

Date_____

Students attending today_____

_____

Total students_____   Estimated Paycheck _____

Music played in class today_____

Date_____

Students attending today_____

_____

Total students_____   Estimated Paycheck _____

Music played in class today_____

Date_____

Students attending today_____

_____

Total students_____   Estimated Paycheck _____

Music played in class today_____

Date_____

Students attending today_____

_____

Total students_____   Estimated Paycheck _____

Music played in class today_____

Date_____

Students attending today_____

_____

Total students_____   Estimated Paycheck _____

Music played in class today_____

Date_____

Students attending today_____

_____

Total students_____   Estimated Paycheck _____

Music played in class today_____

Date_____

Students attending today_____

_____

Total students_____   Estimated Paycheck _____

Music played in class today_____

Date_____

Students attending today_____

_____

Total students_____   Estimated Paycheck _____

Music played in class today_____

Date_____

Students attending today_____

_____

Total students_____   Estimated Paycheck _____

Music played in class today_____

Date_____

Students attending today_____

_____

Total students_____   Estimated Paycheck _____

Music played in class today_____

Date_____

Students attending today_____

_____

Total students_____   Estimated Paycheck _____

Music played in class today_____

Date_____

Students attending today_____

_____

Total students_____   Estimated Paycheck _____

Music played in class today_____

Date_____

Students attending today_____

_____

Total students_____   Estimated Paycheck _____

Music played in class today_____

Date_____

Students attending today_____

_____

Total students_____   Estimated Paycheck _____

Music played in class today_____

Date_____

Students attending today_____

_____

Total students_____   Estimated Paycheck _____

Music played in class today_____

Date_____

Students attending today_____

_____

Total students_____   Estimated Paycheck _____

Music played in class today_____

Date_____

Students attending today_____

_____

Total students_____   Estimated Paycheck _____

Music played in class today_____

Date_____

Students attending today_____

_____

Total students_____   Estimated Paycheck _____

Music played in class today_____

Date_____

Students attending today_____

_____

Total students_____   Estimated Paycheck _____

Music played in class today_____

Date_____

Students attending today_____

_____

Total students_____   Estimated Paycheck _____

Music played in class today_____

Date_____

Students attending today_____

_____

Total students_____   Estimated Paycheck _____

Music played in class today_____

Date_____

Students attending today_____

_____

Total students_____   Estimated Paycheck _____

Music played in class today_____

Date_____

Students attending today_____

_____

Total students_____   Estimated Paycheck _____

Music played in class today_____

Date_____

Students attending today_____

_____

Total students_____   Estimated Paycheck _____

Music played in class today_____

Date_____

Students attending today_____

_____

Total students_____   Estimated Paycheck _____

Music played in class today_____

Date_____

Students attending today_____

_____

Total students_____   Estimated Paycheck _____

Music played in class today_____

Date_____

Students attending today_____

_____

Total students_____   Estimated Paycheck _____

Music played in class today_____

Date_____

Students attending today_____

_____

Total students_____   Estimated Paycheck _____

Music played in class today_____

Date_____

Students attending today_____

_____

Total students_____   Estimated Paycheck _____

Music played in class today_____

Date_____

Students attending today_____

_____

Total students_____   Estimated Paycheck _____

Music played in class today_____

Date_____

Students attending today_____

_____

Total students_____   Estimated Paycheck _____

Music played in class today_____

Date_____

Students attending today_____

_____

Total students_____   Estimated Paycheck _____

Music played in class today_____

Date_____

Students attending today_____

_____

Total students_____   Estimated Paycheck _____

Music played in class today_____

Date_____

Students attending today_____

_____

Total students_____   Estimated Paycheck _____

Music played in class today_____

Date_____

Students attending today_____

_____

Total students_____   Estimated Paycheck _____

Music played in class today_____

Date_____

Students attending today_____

_____

Total students_____   Estimated Paycheck _____

Music played in class today_____

Date_____

Students attending today_____

_____

Total students_____   Estimated Paycheck _____

Music played in class today_____

Date_____

Students attending today_____

_____

Total students_____   Estimated Paycheck _____

Music played in class today_____

Date_____

Students attending today_____

_____

Total students_____   Estimated Paycheck _____

Music played in class today_____

Date_____

Students attending today_____

_____

Total students_____   Estimated Paycheck _____

Music played in class today_____

Date_____

Students attending today_____

_____

Total students_____   Estimated Paycheck _____

Music played in class today_____

Date_____

Students attending today_____

_____

Total students_____   Estimated Paycheck _____

Music played in class today_____

Date_____

Students attending today_____

_____

Total students_____   Estimated Paycheck _____

Music played in class today_____

Date_____

Students attending today_____

_____

Total students_____   Estimated Paycheck _____

Music played in class today_____

Date_____

Students attending today_____

_____

Total students_____   Estimated Paycheck _____

Music played in class today_____

Date_____

Students attending today_____

_____

Total students_____   Estimated Paycheck _____

Music played in class today_____

Date_____

Students attending today_____

_____

Total students_____   Estimated Paycheck _____

Music played in class today_____

Date_____

Students attending today_____

_____

Total students_____   Estimated Paycheck _____

Music played in class today_____

Date_____

Students attending today_____

_____

Total students_____   Estimated Paycheck _____

Music played in class today_____

Date_____

Students attending today_____

_____

Total students_____   Estimated Paycheck _____

Music played in class today_____

Date_____

Students attending today_____

_____

Total students_____   Estimated Paycheck _____

Music played in class today_____

Date_____

Students attending today_____

_____

Total students_____   Estimated Paycheck _____

Music played in class today_____

Date_____

Students attending today_____

_____

Total students_____   Estimated Paycheck _____

Music played in class today_____

Date_____

Students attending today_____

_____

Total students_____   Estimated Paycheck _____

Music played in class today_____

Date_____

Students attending today_____

_____

Total students_____   Estimated Paycheck _____

Music played in class today_____

Date_____

Students attending today_____

_____

Total students_____   Estimated Paycheck _____

Music played in class today_____

Date_____

Students attending today_____

_____

Total students_____   Estimated Paycheck _____

Music played in class today_____

Date_____

Students attending today_____

_____

Total students_____   Estimated Paycheck _____

Music played in class today_____

Date_____

Students attending today_____

_____

Total students_____   Estimated Paycheck _____

Music played in class today_____

Date_____

Students attending today_____

_____

Total students_____   Estimated Paycheck _____

Music played in class today_____

Date_____

Students attending today_____

_____

Total students_____   Estimated Paycheck _____

Music played in class today_____

Date_____

Students attending today_____

_____

Total students_____   Estimated Paycheck _____

Music played in class today_____

Date_____

Students attending today_____

_____

Total students_____   Estimated Paycheck _____

Music played in class today_____

Date_____

Students attending today_____

_____

Total students_____   Estimated Paycheck _____

Music played in class today_____

Date_____

Students attending today_____

_____

Total students_____   Estimated Paycheck _____

Music played in class today_____

Date_____

Students attending today_____

_____

Total students_____   Estimated Paycheck _____

Music played in class today_____

Date_____

Students attending today_____

_____

Total students_____   Estimated Paycheck _____

Music played in class today_____

Date_____

Students attending today_____

_____

Total students_____   Estimated Paycheck _____

Music played in class today_____

Date_____

Students attending today_____

_____

Total students_____   Estimated Paycheck _____

Music played in class today_____

Date_____

Students attending today_____

_____

Total students_____   Estimated Paycheck _____

Music played in class today_____

Date_____

Students attending today_____

_____

Total students_____   Estimated Paycheck _____

Music played in class today_____

Date_____

Students attending today_____

_____

Total students_____   Estimated Paycheck _____

Music played in class today_____

Date_____

Students attending today_____

_____

Total students_____   Estimated Paycheck _____

Music played in class today_____

Date_____

Students attending today_____

_____

Total students_____   Estimated Paycheck _____

Music played in class today_____

Date_____

Students attending today_____

_____

Total students_____   Estimated Paycheck _____

Music played in class today_____

Date_____

Students attending today_____

_____

Total students_____   Estimated Paycheck _____

Music played in class today_____

Date_____

Students attending today_____

_____

Total students_____   Estimated Paycheck _____

Music played in class today_____

Date_____

Students attending today_____

_____

Total students_____   Estimated Paycheck _____

Music played in class today_____

Date_____

Students attending today_____

_____

Total students_____   Estimated Paycheck _____

Music played in class today_____

Date_____

Students attending today_____

_____

Total students_____   Estimated Paycheck _____

Music played in class today_____

Date_____

Students attending today_____

_____

Total students_____   Estimated Paycheck _____

Music played in class today_____

Date_____

Students attending today_____

_____

Total students_____   Estimated Paycheck _____

Music played in class today_____

Date_____

Students attending today_____

_____

Total students_____   Estimated Paycheck _____

Music played in class today_____

Date_____

Students attending today_____

_____

Total students_____   Estimated Paycheck _____

Music played in class today _____

Date _____

Students attending today _____

_____

Total students _____   Estimated Paycheck _____

Music played in class today _____

Date _____

Students attending today _____

_____

Total students _____   Estimated Paycheck _____

Music played in class today _____

Date _____

Students attending today _____

_____

Total students _____   Estimated Paycheck _____

Music played in class today _____

Date _____

Students attending today _____

_____

Total students _____   Estimated Paycheck _____

Music played in class today_____

Date_____

Students attending today_____

_____

Total students_____   Estimated Paycheck _____

Music played in class today_____

Date_____

Students attending today_____

_____

Total students_____   Estimated Paycheck _____

Music played in class today_____

Date_____

Students attending today_____

_____

Total students_____   Estimated Paycheck _____

Music played in class today_____

Date_____

Students attending today_____

_____

Total students_____   Estimated Paycheck _____

Music played in class today_____

Date_____

Students attending today_____

_____

Total students_____   Estimated Paycheck _____

Music played in class today_____

Date_____

Students attending today_____

_____

Total students_____   Estimated Paycheck _____

Music played in class today_____

Date_____

Students attending today_____

_____

Total students_____   Estimated Paycheck _____

Music played in class today_____

Date_____

Students attending today_____

_____

Total students_____   Estimated Paycheck _____

Music played in class today_____

Date_____

Students attending today_____

_____

Total students_____   Estimated Paycheck _____

Music played in class today_____

Date_____

Students attending today_____

_____

Total students_____   Estimated Paycheck _____

Music played in class today_____

Date_____

Students attending today_____

_____

Total students_____   Estimated Paycheck _____

Music played in class today_____

Date_____

Students attending today_____

_____

Total students_____   Estimated Paycheck _____

Music played in class today_____

Date_____

Students attending today_____

_____

Total students_____   Estimated Paycheck _____

Music played in class today_____

Date_____

Students attending today_____

_____

Total students_____   Estimated Paycheck _____

Music played in class today_____

Date_____

Students attending today_____

_____

Total students_____   Estimated Paycheck _____

Music played in class today_____

Date_____

Students attending today_____

_____

Total students_____   Estimated Paycheck _____

Music played in class today_____

Date_____

Students attending today_____

_____

Total students_____   Estimated Paycheck_____

Music played in class today_____

Date_____

Students attending today_____

_____

Total students_____   Estimated Paycheck_____

Music played in class today_____

Date_____

Students attending today_____

_____

Total students_____   Estimated Paycheck_____

Music played in class today_____

Date_____

Students attending today_____

_____

Total students_____   Estimated Paycheck_____

Music played in class today_____

Date_____

Students attending today_____

_____

Total students_____   Estimated Paycheck _____

Music played in class today_____

Date_____

Students attending today_____

_____

Total students_____   Estimated Paycheck _____

Music played in class today_____

Date_____

Students attending today_____

_____

Total students_____   Estimated Paycheck _____

Music played in class today_____

Date_____

Students attending today_____

_____

Total students_____   Estimated Paycheck _____

Music played in class today_____

Date_____

Students attending today_____

_____

Total students_____   Estimated Paycheck _____

Music played in class today_____

Date_____

Students attending today_____

_____

Total students_____   Estimated Paycheck _____

Music played in class today_____

Date_____

Students attending today_____

_____

Total students_____   Estimated Paycheck _____

Music played in class today_____

Date_____

Students attending today_____

_____

Total students_____   Estimated Paycheck _____

Music played in class today_____

Date_____

Students attending today_____

_____

Total students_____   Estimated Paycheck _____

Music played in class today_____

Date_____

Students attending today_____

_____

Total students_____   Estimated Paycheck _____

Music played in class today_____

Date_____

Students attending today_____

_____

Total students_____   Estimated Paycheck _____

Music played in class today_____

Date_____

Students attending today_____

_____

Total students_____   Estimated Paycheck _____

Music played in class today_____

Date_____

Students attending today_____

_____

Total students_____   Estimated Paycheck _____

Music played in class today_____

Date_____

Students attending today_____

_____

Total students_____   Estimated Paycheck _____

Music played in class today_____

Date_____

Students attending today_____

_____

Total students_____   Estimated Paycheck _____

Music played in class today_____

Date_____

Students attending today_____

_____

Total students_____   Estimated Paycheck _____

Music played in class today_____

Date_____

Students attending today_____

_____

Total students_____   Estimated Paycheck _____

Music played in class today_____

Date_____

Students attending today_____

_____

Total students_____   Estimated Paycheck _____

Music played in class today_____

Date_____

Students attending today_____

_____

Total students_____   Estimated Paycheck _____

Music played in class today_____

Date_____

Students attending today_____

_____

Total students_____   Estimated Paycheck _____

Music played in class today_____

Date_____

Students attending today_____

_____

Total students_____   Estimated Paycheck _____

Music played in class today_____

Date_____

Students attending today_____

_____

Total students_____   Estimated Paycheck _____

Music played in class today_____

Date_____

Students attending today_____

_____

Total students_____   Estimated Paycheck _____

Music played in class today_____

Date_____

Students attending today_____

_____

Total students_____   Estimated Paycheck _____

Music played in class today_____

Date_____

Students attending today_____

_____

Total students_____   Estimated Paycheck _____

Music played in class today_____

Date_____

Students attending today_____

_____

Total students_____   Estimated Paycheck _____

Music played in class today_____

Date_____

Students attending today_____

_____

Total students_____   Estimated Paycheck _____

Music played in class today_____

Date_____

Students attending today_____

_____

Total students_____   Estimated Paycheck _____

Music played in class today_____

Date_____

Students attending today_____

_____

Total students_____   Estimated Paycheck _____

Music played in class today_____

Date_____

Students attending today_____

_____

Total students_____   Estimated Paycheck _____

Music played in class today_____

Date_____

Students attending today_____

_____

Total students_____   Estimated Paycheck _____

Music played in class today_____

Date_____

Students attending today_____

_____

Total students_____   Estimated Paycheck _____

Music played in class today_____

Date_____

Students attending today_____

_____

Total students_____   Estimated Paycheck _____

Music played in class today_____

Date_____

Students attending today_____

_____

Total students_____   Estimated Paycheck _____

Music played in class today_____

Date_____

Students attending today_____

_____

Total students_____   Estimated Paycheck _____

Music played in class today_____

Date_____

Students attending today_____

_____

Total students_____   Estimated Paycheck _____

Music played in class today_____

Date_____

Students attending today_____

_____

Total students_____   Estimated Paycheck _____

Music played in class today_____

Date_____

Students attending today_____

_____

Total students_____   Estimated Paycheck _____

Music played in class today_____

Date_____

Students attending today_____

_____

Total students_____   Estimated Paycheck _____

Music played in class today_____

Date_____

Students attending today_____

_____

Total students_____   Estimated Paycheck _____

Music played in class today _____

Date _____

Students attending today _____

_____

Total students _____   Estimated Paycheck _____

Music played in class today _____

Date _____

Students attending today _____

_____

Total students _____   Estimated Paycheck _____

Music played in class today _____

Date _____

Students attending today _____

_____

Total students _____   Estimated Paycheck _____

Music played in class today _____

Date _____

Students attending today _____

_____

Total students _____   Estimated Paycheck _____

Music played in class today_____

Date_____

Students attending today_____

_____

Total students_____   Estimated Paycheck _____

Music played in class today_____

Date_____

Students attending today_____

_____

Total students_____   Estimated Paycheck _____

Music played in class today_____

Date_____

Students attending today_____

_____

Total students_____   Estimated Paycheck _____

Music played in class today_____

Date_____

Students attending today_____

_____

Total students_____   Estimated Paycheck _____

Music played in class today _____

Date _____

Students attending today _____

_____

Total students _____   Estimated Paycheck _____

Music played in class today _____

Date _____

Students attending today _____

_____

Total students _____   Estimated Paycheck _____

Music played in class today _____

Date _____

Students attending today _____

_____

Total students _____   Estimated Paycheck _____

Music played in class today _____

Date _____

Students attending today _____

_____

Total students _____   Estimated Paycheck _____

Music played in class today_____

Date_____

Students attending today_____

_____

Total students_____   Estimated Paycheck _____

Adjustments

Add your special adjustments on the next several pages.

Your Adjustments

Your Adjustments

Your Adjustments

Your Adjustments

Your Adjustments

Your Adjustments

Your Adjustments

Your Adjustments

Your Adjustments

Your Adjustments

Your Adjustments

Your Adjustments

Your Adjustments

Your Adjustments

Student Problem Areas

This page is for your students. I have students who have particular problems. One has back problems, one has shoulder problems, one has carpal tunnel and can't use her hands much. I write down what I have recommended for them and if it works or not. I also use this page to record how to compensate for their particular problem. I try to stretch out the area that hurts and surrounding areas that will ease their pain.

Name of Student_____ Student's Problem_____
Asanas recommended and results

Name of Student_____ Student's Problem_____
Asanas recommended and results

Name of Student_____ Student's Problem_____
Asanas recommended and results

Name of Student_____ Student's Problem_____
Asanas recommended and results

Student Problem Areas

Name of Student_____ Student's Problem_____
Asanas recommended and results

Name of Student_____ Student's Problem_____
Asanas recommended and results

Name of Student_____ Student's Problem_____
Asanas recommended and results

Name of Student_____ Student's Problem_____
Asanas recommended and results

Student Problem Areas

Name of Student_____ Student's Problem_____
Asanas recommended and results

Name of Student_____ Student's Problem_____
Asanas recommended and results

Name of Student_____ Student's Problem_____
Asanas recommended and results

Name of Student_____ Student's Problem_____
Asanas recommended and results

Student Problem Areas

Name of Student_____ Student's Problem_____
Asanas recommended and results

Name of Student_____ Student's Problem_____
Asanas recommended and results

Name of Student_____ Student's Problem_____
Asanas recommended and results

Name of Student_____ Student's Problem_____
Asanas recommended and results

Student Problem Areas

Name of Student_____ Student's Problem_____
Asanas recommended and results

Name of Student_____ Student's Problem_____
Asanas recommended and results

Name of Student_____ Student's Problem_____
Asanas recommended and results

Name of Student_____ Student's Problem_____
Asanas recommended and results

Student Problem Areas

Name of Student_____ Student's Problem_____
Asanas recommended and results

Name of Student_____ Student's Problem_____
Asanas recommended and results

Name of Student_____ Student's Problem_____
Asanas recommended and results

Name of Student_____ Student's Problem_____
Asanas recommended and results

Student Problem Areas

Name of Student_____ Student's Problem_____
Asanas recommended and results

Name of Student_____ Student's Problem_____
Asanas recommended and results

Name of Student_____ Student's Problem_____
Asanas recommended and results

Name of Student_____ Student's Problem_____
Asanas recommended and results

Student Problem Areas

Name of Student_____ Student's Problem_____
Asanas recommended and results

Name of Student_____ Student's Problem_____
Asanas recommended and results

Name of Student_____ Student's Problem_____
Asanas recommended and results

Name of Student_____ Student's Problem_____
Asanas recommended and results

Student Problem Areas

Name of Student_____ Student's Problem_____
Asanas recommended and results

Name of Student_____ Student's Problem_____
Asanas recommended and results

Name of Student_____ Student's Problem_____
Asanas recommended and results

Name of Student_____ Student's Problem_____
Asanas recommended and results

Student Problem Areas

Name of Student_____ Student's Problem_____
Asanas recommended and results

Name of Student_____ Student's Problem_____
Asanas recommended and results

Name of Student_____ Student's Problem_____
Asanas recommended and results

Name of Student_____ Student's Problem_____
Asanas recommended and results

Student Problem Areas

Name of Student_____ Student's Problem_____
Asanas recommended and results

Name of Student_____ Student's Problem_____
Asanas recommended and results

Name of Student_____ Student's Problem_____
Asanas recommended and results

Name of Student_____ Student's Problem_____
Asanas recommended and results

End of Class Poems or Remarks

End of Class Poems or Remarks

End of Class Poems or Remarks

End of Class Poems or Remarks

End of Class Poems or Remarks

End of Class Poems or Remarks

Yoga Cures for Various Problems

My students often ask for yogic cures for their problems. Please remind them to try this at their own risk and state that you are not a doctor.

Allergies -a neti Pot works wonders. Some of my students have an aversion to this and I recommend a saline nasal spray from the drug store. It is a saline spray. Pure saline nothing else is added to the spray it has a spout to go into your nose.

Anxiety/Panic Attack- pranayama will help. I recommend slow deep breaths.

Arthritis -Cure depends on where the problem is. In hands and fingers do finger exercises. (Play the piano, move the fingers and wrist, circle the wrist, etc.)

Asthma - Pranayama

Back pain -depends on where the pain is upper back lower back, scoliosis, lordosis, sciatica. I use setu bandha sarvangasana, twists, cat stretches, bhujangasana. (Always consider the location of the pain as some asanas will not be helpful.)

Constipation/Upset stomach - Nauli, Seated Twist, lying twist
Move the digestive organs helping move everything through the system.

Depression - Legs up the wall, headstand, shoulder stand or any inversion. All improved blood flow to the brain. Avoid meditation.

Digestion - any twist

Headache -Legs up the wall or headstand as long as there is not detached retina or hypertension.

Hypertension -Savasama, **no inversions**, including downward dog.

Improve Memory –Two minutes a day of any inversion will improve memory. All improve blood flow to the brain.

Insomnia – long slow pranayama, savasana, propped up in bolsters, or in bed.

Jet Lag –Savasana, propped up in bolsters, or in bed.

PART THREE

Workshops You Attend

Name of Workshop
Presenters
Topics Covered
Date
C.E.U.'s Earned
Certificate Earned?

Name of Workshop
Presenters
Topics Covered
Date
C.E.U.'s Earned
Certificate Earned?

Name of Workshop
Presenters
Topics Covered
Date
C.E.U.'s Earned
Certificate Earned?

Name of Workshop
Presenters
Topics Covered
Date
C.E.U.'s Earned
Certificate Earned?

Name of Workshop
Presenters
Topics Covered
Date
C.E.U.'s Earned
Certificate Earned?
Total C.E.U's Earned _____

Workshops You Attend

Name of Workshop
Presenters
Topics Covered
Date
C.E.U.'s Earned
Certificate Earned?

Name of Workshop
Presenters
Topics Covered
Date
C.E.U.'s Earned
Certificate Earned?

Name of Workshop
Presenters
Topics Covered
Date
C.E.U.'s Earned
Certificate Earned?

Name of Workshop
Presenters
Topics Covered
Date
C.E.U.'s Earned
Certificate Earned?

Name of Workshop
Presenters
Topics Covered
Date
Certificate Earned?
C.E.U.'s Earned
Total C.E.U's Earned _____

Workshops You Attend

Name of Workshop
Presenters
Topics Covered
Date
C.E.U.'s Earned
Certificate Earned?

Name of Workshop
Presenters
Topics Covered
Date
C.E.U.'s Earned
Certificate Earned?

Name of Workshop
Presenters
Topics Covered
Date
C.E.U.'s Earned
Certificate Earned?

Name of Workshop
Presenters
Topics Covered
Date
C.E.U.'s Earned
Certificate Earned?

Name of Workshop
Presenters
Topics Covered
Date
Certificate Earned?
C.E.U.'s Earned
Total C.E.U's Earned _____

Workshops You Attend

Name of Workshop
Presenters
Topics Covered
Date
C.E.U.'s Earned
Certificate Earned?

Name of Workshop
Presenters
Topics Covered
Date
C.E.U.'s Earned
Certificate Earned?

Name of Workshop
Presenters
Topics Covered
Date
C.E.U.'s Earned
Certificate Earned?

Name of Workshop
Presenters
Topics Covered
Date
C.E.U.'s Earned
Certificate Earned?

Name of Workshop
Presenters
Topics Covered
Date
Certificate Earned?
C.E.U.'s Earned
Total C.E.U's Earned _____

Workshops You Attend

Name of Workshop
Presenters
Topics Covered
Date
C.E.U.'s Earned
Certificate Earned?

Name of Workshop
Presenters
Topics Covered
Date
C.E.U.'s Earned
Certificate Earned?

Name of Workshop
Presenters
Topics Covered
Date
C.E.U.'s Earned
Certificate Earned?

Name of Workshop
Presenters
Topics Covered
Date
C.E.U.'s Earned
Certificate Earned?

Name of Workshop
Presenters
Topics Covered
Date
Certificate Earned?
C.E.U.'s Earned
Total C.E.U's Earned _____

Workshops You Attend

Name of Workshop
Presenters
Topics Covered
Date
C.E.U.'s Earned
Certificate Earned?

Name of Workshop
Presenters
Topics Covered
Date
C.E.U.'s Earned
Certificate Earned?

Name of Workshop
Presenters
Topics Covered
Date
C.E.U.'s Earned
Certificate Earned?

Name of Workshop
Presenters
Topics Covered
Date
C.E.U.'s Earned
Certificate Earned?

Name of Workshop
Presenters
Topics Covered
Date
Certificate Earned?
C.E.U.'s Earned
Total C.E.U's Earned _____

A new way to take notes

The Cornell Method of note taking

To use this method of note taking you must draw a vertical line down the paper the left side list the important points. (Summary of important points) The right side you take your normal notes. I have used this method and I find it helpful. It teaches you to organize your notes.
I normally rewrite my notes using this method. If I draw yoga stick figures, I draw them to the right. Use abbreviations where possible it saves time. Review and rewrite your notes if necessary.

Example of how your page should look. On 8x5 paper

Main Ideas   Central Notes
2.5"   6"

Summaries of the notes above
2"

New Asanas you have borrowed from classes or workshops

New Asanas you have borrowed from classes or workshops

New Asanas you have borrowed from classes or workshops

New Asanas you have borrowed from classes or workshops

New Asanas you have borrowed from classes or workshops

New Asanas you have borrowed from classes or workshops

New Asanas you have borrowed from classes or workshops

Classes/Workshop Notes

Classes/Workshop Notes

Classes/Workshop Notes

Classes/Workshop Notes

Classes/Workshop Notes

Classes/Workshop Notes

Classes/Workshop Notes

Classes/Workshop Notes

Classes/Workshop Notes

Classes/Workshop Notes

Classes/Workshop Notes

Classes/Workshop Notes

Classes/Workshop Notes

Classes/Workshop Notes

Classes/Workshop Notes

Classes/Workshop Notes

Classes/Workshop Notes

Classes/Workshop Notes

Classes/Workshop Notes

Classes/Workshop Notes

Classes/Workshop Notes

Classes/Workshop Notes

Classes I Like

Place
Time
Date
Phone number
Instructor
What I like most

Place
Time
Date
Phone number
Instructor
What I like most

Place
Time
Date
Phone number
Instructor
What I like most

Place
Time
Date
Phone number
Instructor
What I like most

Classes I Like

Place
Time
Date
Phone number
Instructor
What I like most

Place
Time
Date
Phone number
Instructor
What I like most

Place
Time
Date
Phone number
Instructor
What I like most

Place
Time
Date
Phone number
Instructor
What I like most

Classes I Like

Place
Time
Date
Phone number
Instructor
What I like most

Place
Time
Date
Phone number
Instructor
What I like most

Place
Time
Date
Phone number
Instructor
What I like most

Place
Time
Date
Phone number
Instructor
What I like most

Your Yoga Practice

Example

Date

Pranayama Abdominal breathing
Meditation Metta

Asana what I worked on: Hip Openers (etc.)

What I want to work on next time Back bends

Savasana/Restorative yoga propped on bolster 20 min.

Date_____

Pranayama_____

Meditation_____

Asana what I worked on_____

What I want to work on next time_____

Savasana/Restorative yoga_____

Date_____

Pranayama_____

Meditation_____

Asana what I worked on_____

What I want to work on next time_____

Savasana/Restorative yoga_____

Yoga Practice

Date_____

Pranayama_____

Meditation_____

Asana what I worked on_____

What I want to work on next time_____

Savasana/Restorative yoga_____

Date_____

Pranayama_____

Meditation_____

Asana what I worked on_____

What I want to work on next time_____

Savasana/Restorative yoga_____

Date_____

Pranayama_____

Meditation_____

Asana what I worked on_____

What I want to work on next time_____

Savasana/Restorative yoga_____

Yoga Practice

Date_____

Pranayama_____

Meditation_____

Asana what I worked on_____

What I want to work on next time_____

Savasana/Restorative yoga_____

Date_____

Pranayama_____

Meditation_____

Asana what I worked on_____

What I want to work on next time_____

Savasana/Restorative yoga_____

Date_____

Pranayama_____

Meditation_____

Asana what I worked on_____

What I want to work on next time_____

Savasana/Restorative yoga_____

Yoga Practice

Date_____

Pranayama_____

Meditation_____

Asana what I worked on_____

What I want to work on next time_____

Savasana/Restorative yoga_____

Date_____

Pranayama_____

Meditation_____

Asana what I worked on_____

What I want to work on next time_____

Savasana/Restorative yoga_____

Date_____

Pranayama_____

Meditation_____

Asana what I worked on_____

What I want to work on next time_____

Savasana/Restorative yoga_____

Yoga Practice

Date_____

Pranayama_____

Meditation_____

Asana what I worked on_____

What I want to work on next time_____

Savasana/Restorative yoga_____

Date_____

Pranayama_____

Meditation_____

Asana what I worked on_____

What I want to work on next time_____

Savasana/Restorative yoga_____

Date_____

Pranayama_____

Meditation_____

Asana what I worked on_____

What I want to work on next time_____

Savasana/Restorative yoga_____

Yoga Practice

Date_____

Pranayama_____

Meditation_____

Asana what I worked on_____

What I want to work on next time_____

Savasana/Restorative yoga_____

Date_____

Pranayama_____

Meditation_____

Asana what I worked on_____

What I want to work on next time_____

Savasana/Restorative yoga_____

Date_____

Pranayama_____

Meditation_____

Asana what I worked on_____

What I want to work on next time_____

Savasana/Restorative yoga_____

Yoga Practice

Date_____

Pranayama_____

Meditation_____

Asana what I worked on_____

What I want to work on next time_____

Savasana/Restorative yoga_____

Date_____

Pranayama_____

Meditation_____

Asana what I worked on_____

What I want to work on next time_____

Savasana/Restorative yoga_____

Date_____

Pranayama_____

Meditation_____

Asana what I worked on_____

What I want to work on next time_____

Savasana/Restorative yoga_____

Yoga Practice

Date_____

Pranayama_____

Meditation_____

Asana what I worked on_____

What I want to work on next time_____

Savasana/Restorative yoga_____

Date_____

Pranayama_____

Meditation_____

Asana what I worked on_____

What I want to work on next time_____

Savasana/Restorative yoga_____

Date_____

Pranayama_____

Meditation_____

Asana what I worked on_____

What I want to work on next time_____

Savasana/Restorative yoga_____

Yoga Practice

Date_____

Pranayama_____

Meditation_____

Asana what I worked on_____

What I want to work on next time_____

Savasana/Restorative yoga_____

Date_____

Pranayama_____

Meditation_____

Asana what I worked on_____

What I want to work on next time_____

Savasana/Restorative yoga_____

Date_____

Pranayama_____

Meditation_____

Asana what I worked on_____

What I want to work on next time_____

Savasana/Restorative yoga_____

Yoga Practice

Date_____

Pranayama_____

Meditation_____

Asana what I worked on_____

What I want to work on next time_____

Savasana/Restorative yoga_____

Date_____

Pranayama_____

Meditation_____

Asana what I worked on_____

What I want to work on next time_____

Savasana/Restorative yoga_____

Date_____

Pranayama_____

Meditation_____

Asana what I worked on_____

What I want to work on next time_____

Savasana/Restorative yoga_____

Yoga Practice

Date_____

Pranayama_____

Meditation_____

Asana what I worked on_____

What I want to work on next time_____

Savasana/Restorative yoga_____

Date_____

Pranayama_____

Meditation_____

Asana what I worked on_____

What I want to work on next time_____

Savasana/Restorative yoga_____

Date_____

Pranayama_____

Meditation_____

Asana what I worked on_____

What I want to work on next time_____

Savasana/Restorative yoga_____

Yoga Practice

Date_____

Pranayama_____

Meditation_____

Asana what I worked on_____

What I want to work on next time_____

Savasana/Restorative yoga_____

Date_____

Pranayama_____

Meditation_____

Asana what I worked on_____

What I want to work on next time_____

Savasana/Restorative yoga_____

Date_____

Pranayama_____

Meditation_____

Asana what I worked on_____

What I want to work on next time_____

Savasana/Restorative yoga_____

Yoga Practice

Date_____

Pranayama_____

Meditation_____

Asana what I worked on_____

What I want to work on next time_____

Savasana/Restorative yoga_____

Date_____

Pranayama_____

Meditation_____

Asana what I worked on_____

What I want to work on next time_____

Savasana/Restorative yoga_____

Date_____

Pranayama_____

Meditation_____

Asana what I worked on_____

What I want to work on next time_____

Savasana/Restorative yoga_____

Yoga Practice

Date_____

Pranayama_____

Meditation_____

Asana what I worked on_____

What I want to work on next time_____

Savasana/Restorative yoga_____

Date_____

Pranayama_____

Meditation_____

Asana what I worked on_____

What I want to work on next time_____

Savasana/Restorative yoga_____

Date_____

Pranayama_____

Meditation_____

Asana what I worked on_____

What I want to work on next time_____

Savasana/Restorative yoga_____

Yoga Practice

Date_____

Pranayama_____

Meditation_____

Asana what I worked on_____

What I want to work on next time_____

Savasana/Restorative yoga_____

Date_____

Pranayama_____

Meditation_____

Asana what I worked on_____

What I want to work on next time_____

Savasana/Restorative yoga_____

Date_____

Pranayama_____

Meditation_____

Asana what I worked on_____

What I want to work on next time_____

Savasana/Restorative yoga_____

Yoga Practice

Date_____

Pranayama_____

Meditation_____

Asana what I worked on_____

What I want to work on next time_____

Savasana/Restorative yoga_____

Date_____

Pranayama_____

Meditation_____

Asana what I worked on_____

What I want to work on next time_____

Savasana/Restorative yoga_____

Date_____

Pranayama_____

Meditation_____

Asana what I worked on_____

What I want to work on next time_____

Savasana/Restorative yoga_____

Yoga Practice

Date_____

Pranayama_____

Meditation_____

Asana what I worked on_____

What I want to work on next time_____

Savasana/Restorative yoga_____

Date_____

Pranayama_____

Meditation_____

Asana what I worked on_____

What I want to work on next time_____

Savasana/Restorative yoga_____

Date_____

Pranayama_____

Meditation_____

Asana what I worked on_____

What I want to work on next time_____

Savasana/Restorative yoga_____

Yoga Practice

Date_____

Pranayama_____

Meditation_____

Asana what I worked on_____

What I want to work on next time_____

Savasana/Restorative yoga_____

Date_____

Pranayama_____

Meditation_____

Asana what I worked on_____

What I want to work on next time_____

Savasana/Restorative yoga_____

Date_____

Pranayama_____

Meditation_____

Asana what I worked on_____

What I want to work on next time_____

Savasana/Restorative yoga_____

Yoga Practice

Date_____

Pranayama_____

Meditation_____

Asana what I worked on_____

What I want to work on next time_____

Savasana/Restorative yoga_____

Date_____

Pranayama_____

Meditation_____

Asana what I worked on_____

What I want to work on next time_____

Savasana/Restorative yoga_____

Date_____

Pranayama_____

Meditation_____

Asana what I worked on_____

What I want to work on next time_____

Savasana/Restorative yoga_____

Yoga Practice

Date_____

Pranayama_____

Meditation_____

Asana what I worked on_____

What I want to work on next time_____

Savasana/Restorative yoga_____

Date_____

Pranayama_____

Meditation_____

Asana what I worked on_____

What I want to work on next time_____

Savasana/Restorative yoga_____

Date_____

Pranayama_____

Meditation_____

Asana what I worked on_____

What I want to work on next time_____

Savasana/Restorative yoga_____

Yoga Practice

Date_____

Pranayama_____

Meditation_____

Asana what I worked on_____

What I want to work on next time_____

Savasana/Restorative yoga_____

Date_____

Pranayama_____

Meditation_____

Asana what I worked on_____

What I want to work on next time_____

Savasana/Restorative yoga_____

Date_____

Pranayama_____

Meditation_____

Asana what I worked on_____

What I want to work on next time_____

Savasana/Restorative yoga_____

Yoga Practice

Date_____

Pranayama_____

Meditation_____

Asana what I worked on_____

What I want to work on next time_____

Savasana/Restorative yoga_____

Date_____

Pranayama_____

Meditation_____

Asana what I worked on_____

What I want to work on next time_____

Savasana/Restorative yoga_____

Date_____

Pranayama_____

Meditation_____

Asana what I worked on_____

What I want to work on next time_____

Savasana/Restorative yoga_____

Yoga Practice

Date_____

Pranayama_____

Meditation_____

Asana what I worked on_____

What I want to work on next time_____

Savasana/Restorative yoga_____

Date_____

Pranayama_____

Meditation_____

Asana what I worked on_____

What I want to work on next time_____

Savasana/Restorative yoga_____

Date_____

Pranayama_____

Meditation_____

Asana what I worked on_____

What I want to work on next time_____

Savasana/Restorative yoga_____

Yoga Practice

Date_____

Pranayama_____

Meditation_____

Asana what I worked on_____

What I want to work on next time_____

Savasana/Restorative yoga_____

Date_____

Pranayama_____

Meditation_____

Asana what I worked on_____

What I want to work on next time_____

Savasana/Restorative yoga_____

Date_____

Pranayama_____

Meditation_____

Asana what I worked on_____

What I want to work on next time_____

Savasana/Restorative yoga_____

Yoga Practice

Date_____

Pranayama_____

Meditation_____

Asana what I worked on_____

What I want to work on next time_____

Savasana/Restorative yoga_____

Date_____

Pranayama_____

Meditation_____

Asana what I worked on_____

What I want to work on next time_____

Savasana/Restorative yoga_____

Date_____

Pranayama_____

Meditation_____

Asana what I worked on_____

What I want to work on next time_____

Savasana/Restorative yoga_____

Yoga Practice

Date_____

Pranayama_____

Meditation_____

Asana what I worked on_____

What I want to work on next time_____

Savasana/Restorative yoga_____

Date_____

Pranayama_____

Meditation_____

Asana what I worked on_____

What I want to work on next time_____

Savasana/Restorative yoga_____

Date_____

Pranayama_____

Meditation_____

Asana what I worked on_____

What I want to work on next time_____

Savasana/Restorative yoga_____

Yoga Practice

Date_____

Pranayama_____

Meditation_____

Asana what I worked on_____

What I want to work on next time_____

Savasana/Restorative yoga_____

Date_____

Pranayama_____

Meditation_____

Asana what I worked on_____

What I want to work on next time_____

Savasana/Restorative yoga_____

Date_____

Pranayama_____

Meditation_____

Asana what I worked on_____

What I want to work on next time_____

Savasana/Restorative yoga_____

Yoga Practice

Date_____

Pranayama_____

Meditation_____

Asana what I worked on_____

What I want to work on next time_____

Savasana/Restorative yoga_____

Date_____

Pranayama_____

Meditation_____

Asana what I worked on_____

What I want to work on next time_____

Savasana/Restorative yoga_____

Date_____

Pranayama_____

Meditation_____

Asana what I worked on_____

What I want to work on next time_____

Savasana/Restorative yoga_____

Yoga Practice

Date_____

Pranayama_____

Meditation_____

Asana what I worked on_____

What I want to work on next time_____

Savasana/Restorative yoga_____

Date_____

Pranayama_____

Meditation_____

Asana what I worked on_____

What I want to work on next time_____

Savasana/Restorative yoga_____

Date_____

Pranayama_____

Meditation_____

Asana what I worked on_____

What I want to work on next time_____

Savasana/Restorative yoga_____

Yoga Practice

Date_____

Pranayama_____

Meditation_____

Asana what I worked on_____

What I want to work on next time_____

Savasana/Restorative yoga_____

Date_____

Pranayama_____

Meditation_____

Asana what I worked on_____

What I want to work on next time_____

Savasana/Restorative yoga_____

Date_____

Pranayama_____

Meditation_____

Asana what I worked on_____

What I want to work on next time_____

Savasana/Restorative yoga_____

Yoga Practice

Date_____

Pranayama_____

Meditation_____

Asana what I worked on_____

What I want to work on next time_____

Savasana/Restorative yoga_____

Date_____

Pranayama_____

Meditation_____

Asana what I worked on_____

What I want to work on next time_____

Savasana/Restorative yoga_____

Date_____

Pranayama_____

Meditation_____

Asana what I worked on_____

What I want to work on next time_____

Savasana/Restorative yoga_____

Yoga Practice

Date_____

Pranayama_____

Meditation_____

Asana what I worked on_____

What I want to work on next time_____

Savasana/Restorative yoga_____

Date_____

Pranayama_____

Meditation_____

Asana what I worked on_____

What I want to work on next time_____

Savasana/Restorative yoga_____

Date_____

Pranayama_____

Meditation_____

Asana what I worked on_____

What I want to work on next time_____

Savasana/Restorative yoga_____

Yoga Practice

Date_____

Pranayama_____

Meditation_____

Asana what I worked on_____

What I want to work on next time_____

Savasana/Restorative yoga_____

Date_____

Pranayama_____

Meditation_____

Asana what I worked on_____

What I want to work on next time_____

Savasana/Restorative yoga_____

Date_____

Pranayama_____

Meditation_____

Asana what I worked on_____

What I want to work on next time_____

Savasana/Restorative yoga_____

Yoga Practice

Date_____

Pranayama_____

Meditation_____

Asana what I worked on_____

What I want to work on next time_____

Savasana/Restorative yoga_____

Date_____

Pranayama_____

Meditation_____

Asana what I worked on_____

What I want to work on next time_____

Savasana/Restorative yoga_____

Date_____

Pranayama_____

Meditation_____

Asana what I worked on_____

What I want to work on next time_____

Savasana/Restorative yoga_____

Yoga Practice

Date_____

Pranayama_____

Meditation_____

Asana what I worked on_____

What I want to work on next time_____

Savasana/Restorative yoga_____

Date_____

Pranayama_____

Meditation_____

Asana what I worked on_____

What I want to work on next time_____

Savasana/Restorative yoga_____

Date_____

Pranayama_____

Meditation_____

Asana what I worked on_____

What I want to work on next time_____

Savasana/Restorative yoga_____

Yoga Practice

Date_____

Pranayama_____

Meditation_____

Asana what I worked on_____

What I want to work on next time_____

Savasana/Restorative yoga_____

Date_____

Pranayama_____

Meditation_____

Asana what I worked on_____

What I want to work on next time_____

Savasana/Restorative yoga_____

Date_____

Pranayama_____

Meditation_____

Asana what I worked on_____

What I want to work on next time_____

Savasana/Restorative yoga_____

Telephone Book

Name
Home phone
Cell phone
Work phone
Address
Email

Name
Home phone
Cell phone
Work phone
Address
Email

Name
Home phone
Cell phone
Work phone
Address
Email

Name
Home phone
Cell phone
Work phone
Address
Email

Name
Home phone
Cell phone
Work phone
Address
Email

Telephone Book

Name
Home phone
Cell phone
Work phone
Address
Email

Name
Home phone
Cell phone
Work phone
Address
Email

Name
Home phone
Cell phone
Work phone
Address
Email

Name
Home phone
Cell phone
Work phone
Address
Email

Name
Home phone
Cell phone
Work phone
Address
Email

Telephone Book

Name
Home phone
Cell phone
Work phone
Address
Email

Name
Home phone
Cell phone
Work phone
Address
Email

Name
Home phone
Cell phone
Work phone
Address
Email

Name
Home phone
Cell phone
Work phone
Address
Email

Name
Home phone
Cell phone
Work phone
Address
Email

Telephone Book

Name
Home phone
Cell phone
Work phone
Address
Email

Name
Home phone
Cell phone
Work phone
Address
Email

Name
Home phone
Cell phone
Work phone
Address
Email

Name
Home phone
Cell phone
Work phone
Address
Email

Name
Home phone
Cell phone
Work phone
Address
Email

Notes

Notes

Notes

Notes

Notes

Notes

Notes

Notes

About April

I practiced meditation at an early age to deal with the pain of a hereditary illness. Yoga soon followed. I have studied with various yogis all over the planet, as a military wife. I moved every 2-3 years and during that time studied several types of yoga.

When my husband would transfer from one military base to another, I often had to study a different type of yoga, because what I was studying was not offered in the new location. Sometimes I would find one style of yoga more intriguing than another and would study more than one style at a time. I studied Iyengar, Viniyoga, Integrative yoga therapy, Hatha, White lotus, Jivamukti, and several other types of yoga. My yoga is a blend of all of the different types of yoga I have studied. I call it Peaceful Lotus. My goal at Peaceful Lotus is self reflection and self realization following the eight limbs of yoga. This allows the student to work at a pace that is comfortable for each individual. I teach yoga based on healing. All yoga is healing, but I focus on healing dis-ease. With Peaceful Lotus Flows, pranayama, and restorative yoga, it allows the student to inquire within to the root of the dis-ease. And take back their instinctive body knowledge. I am a Yoga Alliance Registered Teacher. I currently have a 500 hour, and an E200 registration. I have studied Sanskrit, and have published two books on yoga and a teacher training manual. I am a reiki master, and I am certified in Qigong. I own Peaceful Lotus teacher training to teach other yogis to be yoga teachers. **I am available for workshops and book signings.**

Please tell me what would you like to see in this book? What did I miss? What would you like changed?

Email me with your thoughts.
In the subject line of the email please put changes to YJY
Check the website for updated versions of this book.

peacefulotus@yahoo.com or hastyfar@yahoo.com

Namaste`

April

978-0-595-37282-9
0-595-37282-1

Printed in the United Kingdom by
Lightning Source UK Ltd., Milton Keynes
139777UK00001B/163/A